Plant Growth and Development

TEXAS PARKS AND WILDLIFE

National Science Resources Center

THE NATIONAL ACADEMIES Smithsonian Institution

THE NATIONAL SCIENCE RESOURCES CENTER (NSRC) was established in 1985 by the Smithsonian Institution and the National Academies to improve the learning and teaching of science for all students in the United States and throughout the world. The prestige and credibility of these two world-renowned institutions provide the NSRC with access to research, scientific expertise, and resources to inform our work, as well as an opportunity to engage and catalyze educators, business people, and scientists in all aspects of science education reform.

THE SMITHSONIAN INSTITUTION was established in 1846 with a mission of increasing and diffusing knowledge. For 160 years, the Smithsonian has used its unique, publicly accessible collections, research, and staff to inform, educate, and inspire a diverse public. In doing this, it has become one of the most widely recognized institutions in the world for both its contributions to science and its unparalleled ability to make its research and collections accessible to people of all ages.

THE NATIONAL ACADEMIES are composed of three academies—the National Academy of Sciences, the National Academy of Engineering, the Institute of Medicine—and their operating arm, the National Research Council. These institutions work outside the framework of government to ensure independent advice to the nation on matters of science, technology, and medicine.

The NSRC advances the missions of its parent institutions by expanding and extending their important work in the following ways:

- Making their work accessible by translating research into products and services for education leaders.
- Building leadership capacity, especially within the science and engineering communities, to leverage change at the school district and state levels.
- Educating a broad constituency of practitioners about the important work of both institutions in science education.

This book is one of a series designed to be an integral component of the Science and Technology for Children® (STC®) curriculum, a research-based, inquiry-centered science program for children in kindergarten through grade six. This program would not have been possible without the generous support of federal agencies, private foundations, and corporations. Supporters include the National Science Foundation, the Smithsonian Institution, the U.S. Department of Defense, the U.S. Department of Education, the John D. and Catherine T. MacArthur Foundation, the Dow Chemical Company Foundation, the Amoco Foundation, Inc., DuPont, the Hewlett-Packard Company, the Smithsonian Institution Educational Outreach Fund, the Smithsonian Women's Committee, and a W.K. Kellogg grant administered by the National Academies.

Acknowledgments

PLANT GROWTH AND DEVELOPMENT is part of a series of books for students in kindergarten through sixth grade, and it is an integral part of the Science and Technology for Children® (STC®) curriculum program. The purpose of these books is to enhance and extend STC's inquiry-based investigations through reading. Research has shown that students improve their reading skills when challenged with interesting and engaging reading materials. In the process, key science concepts that students have been learning can be reinforced. The Teacher's Guide that accompanies the STC program gives some information on how to integrate this book with the program's inquiry-centered investigations. Those students interested in reading these books on their own will find them easy to read as stand-alone texts. Students will especially enjoy reading about highlights of the Smithsonian Institution's varied and unique museums and research facilities.

The book has undergone rigorous review by experts in the field to ensure that all the information is current and accurate. A nationally recognized reading specialist has worked with us to create stories that are at a reading level that is appropriate for students in third grade. We have also varied the reading level throughout the book so that all students—no matter what their reading proficiency—can find stories that are both interesting and challenging.

The NSRC greatly appreciates the efforts of all the individuals listed below. Each contributed his or her expertise to ensure that the book is of the highest quality.

ACKNOWLEDGMENTS

Project Administration

Sally Goetz Shuler
Executive Director
National Science Resources Center

Kimberly Wayman
Financial and Administrative Specialist
National Science Resources Center

Project Management

Claudia Campbell
Senior Research Associate
Managing Editor
National Science Resources Center

Ian MacGregor
Senior Scientist (Consultant)
Napa, California

Barbara Thomas
Director of Communications and
  Publications
Production Manager
National Science Resources Center

Communications and Publications

Barbara Thomas
Director
National Science Resources Center

Jim Benson
Editor
National Science Resources Center

Susan Tannahill
Webmaster and Database Specialist
National Science Resources Center

Heidi Kupke
Publications Technology Specialist
National Science Resources Center

Research and Development Consultants

Lynda DeWitt
Writer (Consultant)
Bethesda, Maryland

Toni Eugene
Writer (Consultant)
Vienna, Virginia

Audrey Huang
Writer (Consultant)
Baltimore, Maryland

Terry Jennings
Writer (Consultant)
Reston, Virginia

Gail Peck
Graphic Designer (Consultant)
Silver Spring, Maryland

Jane Martin
Photo Editor (Consultant)
Arlington, Virginia

Science Literacy Expert

Annemarie Sullivan Palincsar
Jean and Charles Walgreen Professor of
  Reading and Literacy
School of Education
University of Michigan at Ann Arbor

Scientific and Educational Contributors
and Reviewers

David Marsland
Co-Director, Professional Development
  Center
National Science Resources Center

Henry Milne
Co-Director, Professional Development
  Center
National Science Resources Center

Tess Arnold
Owner and Beekeeper
Arnold Honeybee Services
Knoxville, Tennessee

Heather Brown
Chief of Interpretation
Tall Grass Prairie National Preserve
Strong City, Kansas

Kathleen Cullinan
National Program Leader
USDA/CSREES
Washington, D.C.

Bert Drake
Senior Scientist
Smithsonian Environmental Research
  Center
Edgewater, Maryland

Park Staff
George Washington Carver
  National Monument
National Park Service
Diamond, Missouri

Kathryn Kennedy
President and Executive Director
Center for Plant Conservation
Missouri Botanical Garden
St. Louis, Missouri

Beth L. Laube, PhD
Associate Professor
Johns Hopkins University
School of Medicine
Baltimore, Maryland

James H. Miller
Research Ecologist
USDA Forest Service
Auburn, Alabama

Tom Mirenda
Orchid Collection Specialist
Smithsonian Greenhouse Complex
Washington, D.C.

Mario Morales
Medicinal Botanicals Program
Mountain State University
Beckley, West Virginia

Catherine Nagel
Executive Director
National Association for Olmsted Parks
Washington, D.C.

Ken Nagy
Professor Emeritus
Department of Ecology and Evolutionary
  Biology
University of California at Los Angeles

Olav Oftedal
Research Scientist
Species Conservation Center
Smithsonian National Zoological Park
Washington, D.C.

Miles Roberts
Deputy Head
Department of Conservation Biology
Smithsonian National Zoological Park
Washington, D.C.

Liza Stearns
National Park Service
Brookline, Massachusetts

Mary Travaglini
Potomac Gorge Habitat Restoration
  Manager
The Nature Conservancy
Bethesda, Maryland

Jacalyn Willis
Director
Professional Resources in Science and
  Mathematics (PRISM)
Montclair State University
Montclair, New Jersey

Jess Zimmerman
Professor
Institute for Tropical Ecosystem Studies
University of Puerto Rico
San Juan, Puerto Rico

Special thanks to the following schools
in Pennsylvania:

Germantown Friends Academy in
  Germantown
Greenfield Elementary School in
  Philadelphia
Hillsdale Elementary School in West
  Chester
Oak Lane Day School in Norristown
Robeson Elementary School in Birdsboro
St. Basil's Elementary School in
  Kimberton

Plant Growth and Development

CONTENTS

p. 16

p. 28

p. 44

p. 60

ABOVE: (FROM THE TOP) COURTESY OF UNITED STATES DEPARTMENT OF AGRICULTURE; KIMBRA CUTLIP, SMITHSONIAN ENVIRONMENTAL RESEARCH CENTER; COURTESY OF KEN NAGY; THE NATURE CONSERVANCY

COVER: CAROLINA BIOLOGICAL SUPPLY COMPANY (BEE); COURTESY OF UNITED STATES DEPARTMENT OF AGRICULTURE (PRODUCE SECTION); LIBRARY OF CONGRESS (CARVER); VALERIE WRIGHT, KONZA PRAIRIE BIOLOGICAL STATION (PRAIRIE WITH BUTTERFLY MILKWEED—ORANGE FLOWERS)

Introduction

What did you see on the way to school today? You might be thinking of buildings or people. What about grasses, bushes, or trees? Plants are easy to overlook, but they matter. You eat plants, wear plants, and use medicines made of plants. You may enjoy looking at them, or sitting in their shade. In this book, let's take the time to learn more about plants and what they do for us. We'll also meet scientists and other people who work with plants.

Think about the plants in your life. How many plants go into your Thanksgiving dinner? Maybe some of them grow near where you live. Discover where different kinds of plants live and why they live there. Then, visit Central Park in New York City to get to know a landscape architect who thought that making room for plants would make cities better.

Plants need food, water, and protection. But they don't get these things the way you do. For one thing, they don't go to the store for food. They make their own. What do you think plants use to make food? Plants can't run or hide from danger either. Instead, they have other defenses. You've probably seen, felt, or tasted some of them.

Understanding plants can make a difference. Meet an inventor who knew plants and soils. He used his knowledge to help people. Then read about a scientist who studied corn. She learned something exciting, but few other scientists believed her.

Plants and animals depend on each other. When plants make new plants, animals get involved. So do people. Follow a beekeeper to find out how. How else do plants and animals interact? Wrap up by drawing a web of the connections between plants and animals.

Why should we care about plants going extinct? Let's look at a few endangered plants and the people trying to save them. Imagine a place where the grass was as tall as you. Now read about what it was like when that place existed. We'll finish with some reasons why plants die out—including a plant that grows so fast it kills other plants.

If you see this icon in the upper right-hand corner, it's a story about scientists and the work they do.

PART 1

Plants Make Life Possible

Look around you; then close your eyes. Try to imagine life without plants and look again. Plants provide us with food, medicine, and clothing. And they help make our world beautiful.

The stories in this section are:

- Celebrate with Food
- Regions and Seasons
- Natural Medicines
- Tracking New Medicines
- Are You Wearing a Plant?
- Frederick Law Olmsted: The Father of Parks

Frederick Law Olmsted (1822–1903) was a United States landscape architect, famous for designing many well-known city parks and college campuses.

The first two stories are about the different foods that come from plants and where those plants grow. First let's look at the importance of food plants in celebrations. And the next story explains why some plants grow well in some parts of the world but not in others.

The next two stories show the importance of plants as natural medicines and how scientists are working to grow some medicinal plants on farms.

In the fifth story find out how your favorite blue jeans and T-shirts contain strands of cotton plants that have been harvested and woven into cloth.

Finally, read about a man who loved nature and used plants to create parks and to beautify our world.

Celebrate with FOOD

Do you have a favorite meal? Many people think Thanksgiving is the best meal of the year. If you were going to help fix Thanksgiving dinner, what would you serve? Where would you start?

Most of us get our food from the grocery store. But our food doesn't start there. It is grown on farms. Many of our favorite foods are plants or made from plants. Did you know that when you eat some plants, you're eating roots, stems, seeds, leaves, and flowers as well as fruit?

Stems and Seeds

Mashed potatoes or sweet potatoes are often served at a traditional Thanksgiving feast. They are made from the underground stems of plants. Do you remember the story of the first Thanksgiving? The Indians brought the Pilgrims corn. Every kernel in an ear of corn is a seed of a new corn plant. Some other vegetables, such as peas and beans, are also seeds.

The bread on your table comes from plants, too. Wheat, rice, corn, and oats are grains, or seeds from grass plants. ▶

BEN FRASKE, CREATIVE COMMONS ATTRIBUTION SHAREALIKE LICENSE V. 2.5

The centerpiece of today's Thanksgiving in the United States is a large meal that includes a roasted turkey. Many of the dishes in a traditional Thanksgiving meal are made from foods native to North America.

COURTESY OF UNITED STATES DEPARTMENT OF AGRICULTURE

The produce section in a grocery store has many farm-grown foods, especially fruits and vegetables. The produce is often fresh and may come from farms nearby.

When you eat an ear of corn, you are really eating the seeds of a corn plant. Corn was an especially important crop for the American Indians of the New World. Green beans are the unripe pods and seeds of a bean plant. Green beans are sold canned, frozen, and fresh.

(BOTH) COURTESY OF UNITED STATES DEPARTMENT OF AGRICULTURE

Many grains are ground into flour used in baking bread. We eat some grains, such as rice, whole.

Leaves, Fruits, and Flowers

Would you serve salad at your Thanksgiving dinner? Spinach and lettuce are the leaves of the plants. The celery we eat is the stalk of the celery plant. Many of the foods you add to your salad—nuts, tomatoes, broccoli, or cauliflower—also come from plants. Even the salad dressing comes from part of a plant. Salad oils can be made by squeezing olives, ears of corn, or sunflower seeds.

Do you like cranberries or cranberry sauce at Thanksgiving? A cranberry is a fruit, the part of a plant that contains its seeds. Some people like to eat cranberries whole. Others eat cranberries that have been made into a jelly.

Do you have a favorite dessert at Thanksgiving? The fruits of apple trees and pumpkin vines are often baked into pies. The flavor from the beans of the vanilla plant makes vanilla ice cream so tasty. Cinnamon comes from the bark of a tree. Other spices are ground from leaves, such as sage and parsley, and add taste to your Thanksgiving turkey and dressing.

In many places around the world, people have harvest celebrations like Thanksgiving. Does your family or do your friends have a special meal at this time of year? What special foods do they prepare and eat? ■

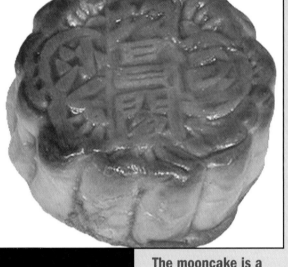

JUNELEE, CREATIVE COMMONS ATTRIBUTION SHAREALIKE 1.0

The mooncake is a traditional Chinese cake eaten during the Mid-Autumn Festival.

SIMON SHEK, CREATIVE COMMONS ATTRIBUTION 2.5 LICENSE

The Mid-Autumn Festival is the most popular Asian celebration of abundance and togetherness, dating back over 3,000 years. Farmers celebrate the end of the summer harvesting season.

Regions and Seasons

There are parts of the world that are known for the food that they grow. For example, the Midwestern United States is sometimes called, "America's Breadbasket," and in Asia, there are fields and fields of rice. To understand how certain foods grow in certain areas of the world, you have to understand climate. Climate is the average weather over a long period of time.

Scientists have divided the world into climate zones according to temperature and rain. The climate map on this page shows seven different climate zones. There are different plants that grow best in each one. Can you find where you live on this climate map?

The colors on this climate zone map show the differences in temperature and rainfall in areas of our world.

Where Food Plants Grow

It's no surprise that the coldest places on Earth are near the North and South Poles. Not many plants can grow in the polar and tundra climates, the PURPLE area on the map, where water is usually frozen. And because of a very short summer, plants grow very slowly. Look for the arid ORANGE areas on the map. These deserts are so hot and dry all year that few food plants can grow there either.

Semi-arid grassland regions, in YELLOW on the map, have cold winters and hot summers with some rain. Farmers can grow lots of grains like wheat and corn in these climate zones. As you read above, so many grains are grown in the Midwestern ▶

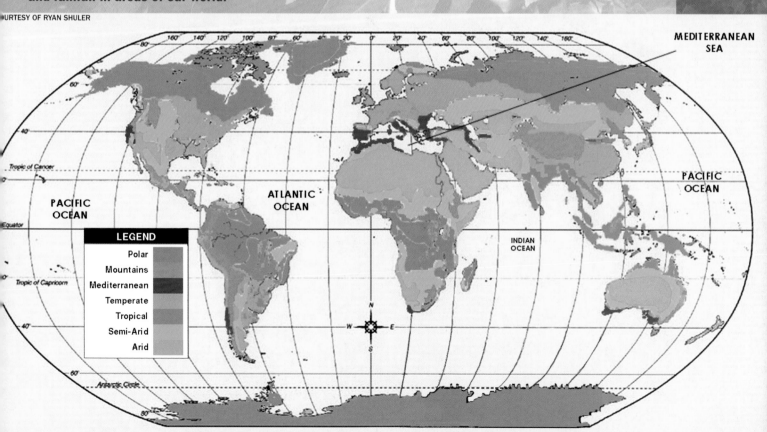

MEDITERRANEAN SEA

PACIFIC OCEAN

ATLANTIC OCEAN

PACIFIC OCEAN

INDIAN OCEAN

Tropic of Cancer

Equator

Tropic of Capricorn

Antarctic Circle

LEGEND	
Polar	
Mountains	
Mediterranean	
Temperate	
Tropical	
Semi-Arid	
Arid	

COURTESY OF UNITED STATES DEPARTMENT OF AGRICULTURE

© DAVID COOK/WWW.BLUESHIFTSTUDIOS.CO.UK/ ALAMY

part of the United States that it is called America's "Breadbasket." You will also find a lot of grains grown in the middle of Europe and Asia. Can you find this area in YELLOW on the climate map?

The BLUE temperate areas have cold winters, warm summers, and enough rain for growing plants. Apples, peaches, and pears grow well in a temperate climate. So do many vegetables, such as peas, carrots, and broccoli. In the warmest parts of temperate climates, farmers can grow oranges, limes, and lemons.

The climate zone with mild and rainy winters followed by hot, dry summers is called Mediterranean RED .

Top of page: Wheat is a cereal grain that is actually a grass and grows well in semi-arid regions worldwide. It is one of the most important food grains in the world, along with rice and corn.

Above: Grapes grow in bunches of 6 to 300 grapes and are most common in the Mediterranean regions of the world. They come in many colors from red to purple to green. You can eat them raw, or use them for making jelly, grape juice, and wine.

Olives and grapes grow well in Mediterranean regions. In the United States, only California has a Mediterranean climate. Strawberries and artichokes also grow well there. What other parts of the world are in the Mediterranean climate zone? Do you have an idea why it is called Mediterranean climate? (Hint: Find the name of the sea near this RED climate zone in Europe.)

Mountain (BROWN) regions are cold all year long and get rain only during the short summers. Potatoes, which grow best where it is cold, are one of the few foods that can be raised in a mountain climate. For more than 7,000 years, people in the mountains of Peru have been growing potatoes for food.

The tropics, the GREEN regions near the equator, are hot all year long. You won't find any snow or ice here, except at the tops of mountains. Farmers need a tropical climate to raise plants that need a lot of water and a long time to grow. Bananas and mangoes are some of the foods that grow best in tropical regions. In the tropical zones in Africa and Asia, rice grows well and is an important food. Do you know what farmers grow where you live? How can you find out? ■

Potatoes are one of the world's most favorite crops grown in mountain regions. They are the fourth largest food crop after rice, wheat, and corn.

Bananas are grown in the tropical climates in more than 120 countries worldwide, more than any other fruit crop.

Natural Medicines

When you get sick, many kinds of medicines can help make you well. But have you ever wondered how sick people got well hundreds of years ago? People then did not have all the medicines we have today. They had to rely on plants.

How do you think they figured out what plants would make good medicines? They had to try many different kinds of plants to find out. Some plants made people sicker, and some did not help at all. Every once in a while, though, a plant cured someone. People remembered that plant and used it from then on.

Quinine as a Cure

Many hundreds of years ago, Indians in the mountains of South America discovered a plant that produced a very important medicine. They used the bark of a small tree called the cinchona (say: sing-KOH-nuh) to bring down fevers. One story tells that the Indians discovered the healing power of cinchona by watching wild cats called jaguars. The jaguars cured themselves of fevers by chewing on

Cinchona officinalis Hook. fil.

Above: A tree native to the Amazon Rainforest, the cinchona plant is used for the production of quinine, which is an anti-fever agent especially useful in the prevention and treatment of malaria.

Left: *Cinchona officinalis L.* is the scientific name for the cinchona plant shown in this drawing.

cinchona trees. The Indians decided to try cinchona, too. They dried the bark and ground it into a white powder. They called the powder "quinine," (say: kwy-nine) which meant "medicine of medicines" in their language.

When Europeans explored South America more than 300 years ago, they learned about quinine and cinchona bark from Peruvian Indians. It was used to fight fevers and a disease called malaria. The explorers took cinchona bark back to Europe where malaria was killing thousands of people every year. Quinine became the best and most well-known cure for malaria.

More Medicinal Plants

You may be surprised to learn how many plants give us medicine. Think of the dandelions you see in some yards. They are not just weeds. Native Americans, Europeans, and the Chinese have used dandelion roots and leaves for hundreds of years to treat swelling, skin problems, and upset stomachs. Aspirin, which relieves the pain of a toothache or pulled muscle, came from the bark of willow trees. Many important medicines used today first came from plants.

Remember, though, it is not safe for you to eat plants that you do not know, since many plants can make you very sick. Leave the experiments to the scientists in laboratories. ■

© FOODCOLLECTION.COM/ALAMY

This photo shows a mortar and pestle that is used to grind and mix substances. The pestle is a heavy stick whose end is used for pounding and grinding, and the mortar is like a bowl.

MARY ELLEN (MEL) HARTE, BUGWOOD.ORG, USDA FOREST SERVICE

Dandelions are short plants with bright yellow flowers. The flowers become round and white with many fluffy fruits we call "seeds." Have you ever picked one and blown the "seeds" into the wind?

Tracking New Medicines

Did you know that some plants use "chemical warfare" to defend themselves from animals that might try to eat them? The chemicals that make up the plant might taste bad. Or they might make the animal sick. But small doses of some of those chemicals might also make good medicines.

Scientists study plants because they are looking for new medicines that cure illnesses and save lives. One of the best medicines for fighting cancer comes from the bark of the yew tree. Scientists found this medicine only about 15 years ago.

Scientists also study ways to grow plants on farms or garden plots so that there will be enough medicine for everyone. One of these scientists is Dr. Mario Morales.

Morales is director of the Medicinal Botanicals Program at Mountain State University in West Virginia. The program gives college courses about medicinal plants and helps people in the community learn more about them.

Doctor of Plants

How did Morales become interested in medicinal plants? He spent his early years on a big coffee farm in Guatemala, a country in Central America. He wandered through the forests and fields picking plants. Workers on the farm helped him identify and learn about the plants he gathered. He remembers people going out to their gardens to pick plants to help cure ailments such as colds, fevers, stomach aches, and headaches. And he remembers people visiting local "healers" to get medicines from plants. Morales learned

Dr. Mario Morales checking a ginseng plant in the Medicinal Plants Garden at Mountain State University at Beckley, West Virginia.

(BOTH) WALTER SIEGMUND, WIKIPEDIA CREATIVE COMMONS ATTRIBUTION 2.5 LICENSE

An important cancer-fighting drug comes from the bark of the Pacific Yew tree. Because of the need for the drug, this tree is becoming a rare plant. Scientists continue to try and produce the drug in laboratories.

DR. MARIO R. MORALES, MEDICINAL BOTANICALS PROGRAM, MOUNTAIN STATE UNIVERSITY, WEST VIRGIN

(BOTH) COURTESY OF UNITED STATES DEPARTMENT OF AGRICULTURE

Above: Goldenseal is easy to identify with its thick, yellow root as well as its large, rounded leaves. It has many uses as a medicinal plant, including treating infections and stomach ache.

Left: A slow growing plant with fleshy roots, ginseng typically grows in cooler climates. Around the world, people grow different kinds of ginseng and use it as a medicine.

a lot about plants' healing powers and went on to universities to learn more.

Today, one of Morales' research projects looks at two plants that grow in the mountains of West Virginia—ginseng and goldenseal. These plants have been used in medicine for hundreds of years. Ginseng has been used by many people for energy and a healthy, long life. Native Americans used goldenseal to dye their clothes and to treat sore gums, and rashes. Goldenseal is also used for treating wounds and infections.

Both plants grow well on the shaded slopes of the West Virginia mountains. And both plants are so popular that they are worth a lot of money. Plant hunters have taken so many ginseng and

goldenseal plants that few of the plants remain in the wild.

Morales and his team are studying how to grow the plants more easily and how to grow more of them. They have found that ginseng and goldenseal grow only where trees provide deep shade. They know that the plants need moist, rich soil. This information will help people who want to domesticate ginseng and goldenseal—that is, grow the plants for human use.

Once ginseng and goldenseal can be domesticated, they will be available at a lower price. People will not have to rely on wild plants to make the medicines they want. Ginseng and goldenseal will be allowed to grow again in the wild. ■

Are You Wearing a Plant?

(ALL) COURTESY OF UNITED STATES DEPARTMENT OF AGRICULTURE

Cotton grows best in areas with a long growing season, plenty of sunshine and water, and dry weather for harvesting. It is a small bush native to tropical and subtropical regions around the world.

What are your favorite clothes? Many people choose blue jeans and T-shirts. These clothes are comfortable because they're made from soft cotton fiber, a material that grows around the seeds of the cotton plant. From the tunics of famous kings of Egypt to your favorite torn jeans, cotton clothing has made people comfortable for thousands of years.

The Fuzz Serves a Purpose

Why do cotton plants grow soft fibers? Each seed of a cotton plant is surrounded by downy fiber and grows inside the seed case of the cotton plant. The case looks a little like a hard brown ball, and when the cottonseeds are ripe, the case pops open. The fluffy cotton fibers act like miniature parachutes for the cottonseeds. When the wind blows, the fibers and seeds float in the air. They can land in a new place where the seeds can grow into a new cotton plant.

Cotton to Cloth

Cotton plants take a long time to produce their fibers, so they mostly grow in areas that are hot or warm most of the year. People in ancient India, Egypt, and Mexico dressed for comfort just as you often do. They were among the first to make cloth

Cotton balls, clothing, and towels are made from the soft fiber that grows around the seeds of the cotton plant.

This picture shows cotton fiber that has been harvested (left) and processed to remove seeds (right).

from cotton. They did all the picking, spinning, and weaving by hand to make the fabric that kept them comfortable.

Today, machines pick the balls of cotton. Other machines remove the seeds, clean the fiber, and spin it into thread. Finally, the thread is woven into fabric for clothing and other products for people around the world. You dry your face on a fluffy cotton towel in the morning, wear comfy jeans in the daytime, and sleep on soft cotton sheets when you go to bed at night.

Look in your closet. Do you still wear all your clothes from last year? Maybe some are too small, and some are out of style. But soft and comfortable cotton will always be popular. ◼

LIBRARY OF CONGRESS

Before there were machines to spin natural fibers into yarn and thread, people did it by hand. This picture from the early 1900s shows a woman using a spinning wheel.

(a) The machinery in this picture is harvesting the fluffy cotton and seeds in a field of cotton plants. Then the cotton is taken to a factory where it is cleaned and processed and spun into thread or yarn.

(b) These jeans were made from a thick cotton cloth called denim, a material that was first used for work clothes. Today, denim is very popular for casual clothing.

COURTESY OF UNITED STATES DEPARTMENT OF AGRICULTURE

a

b

Frederick Law Olmsted:
The Father of Parks

Many years ago, the cities in the United States were quite ugly. They were crowded and unpleasant places to be. One man did extraordinary things to change this. His name was Frederick Law Olmsted, and he became known as the Father of American Landscape Architecture. A landscape architect is a person who plans and designs the use of land.

Olmsted was born almost 200 years ago, when the United States was still very young. His family

New York City in the mid 1800s was crowded and dirty.

(BOTH) LIBRARY OF CONGRESS

was quite wealthy and traveled to many beautiful places. Olmsted decided that all people, not just wealthy people, should be able to enjoy open, green, and peaceful landscapes. He spent his life designing beautiful spaces all over this country.

Frederick Law Olmsted (1822–1903) was a United States landscape architect, famous for designing many well-known city parks and college campuses.

New York's Central Park

There was very little green space in New York City in the mid 1800s. The city had grown so fast that trash and dirt filled the streets. It was crowded, and many people were poor and had nowhere to go. Beggars and robbers wandered the streets. So did horses and cows!

To help solve these problems, New York City set aside more than 840 acres of land in the middle of the city for a park. Olmsted was part of the team selected to

Olmsted helped design and supervise the completion of Central Park in the middle of New York City.

Central Park is a large public, urban park (840 acres or 340 hectares) in New York City. It is the most-visited city park in the United States with about 25 million visitors each year.

design the park. He wanted the park to look as if it had always been there. His design included several ponds where people could boat and skate, squares of green where they could play baseball and badminton. There were groups of trees where people could relax in the shade, and wide, winding paths where they could walk and bike.

It took more than 20 years to build Mr. Olmsted's park. Horse-drawn carts brought in more than ten million loads of dirt and rock. Thousands of workers planted millions of trees, shrubs, and vines. Central Park, as Olmsted had dreamed, became a quiet spot in the middle of New York City. Everyone, from rich to poor, could relax in the park and enjoy the peaceful beauty of nature.

Olmsted's Gift of Green Space

Olmsted continued to plan parks throughout the United States. He also designed the country's first suburbs. Back then, most communities that grew up around a city were laid out in square

blocks. Olmsted planned a community in Illinois that had gently curving streets. He suggested that the houses be set back from the road behind trees. The green spaces in front of the houses were the first yards.

Flowers, leafy trees, and lawns add beauty to our world. Frederick Law Olmsted helped bring these things to all people. It is exciting to think about how one person, who was following his dream, improved the lives of so many people.

Find out more about parks and school campuses designed by Olmsted in your state or area by searching online at the National Association for Olmsted Parks. ■

Following the suggestions of landscape architects like Olmsted, planners design suburbs to include green space with trees and other plants.

Plants Make Life Possible

THAT'S A FACT!
In some parts of the world, quinine is still used for treating malaria, a deadly disease. Quinine comes from the bark of a small tree in South America called the cinchona.

I KNOW THAT!
How do we know about the healing power of some medicinal plants?

WHAT DO YOU THINK?
How many plants and different plant parts have you eaten this week?

HERE'S ONE MORE!
Can you name a famous park that was designed by Frederick Law Olmsted?

PART 2

Plants Are Amazing!

Have you ever noticed how many different-looking plants there are? But even though plants look different, they are the same in many ways. In this book, you will read about the different parts that all plants have and what they do.

In this section:

- It Takes Teamwork
- Getting to the Root of It
- Ouch! That Plant Bit Me!
- Making Food out of Air
- A Farmer's Friend
- A Scientist Who Wouldn't Give Up

The first three stories tell you about the parts of plants and what they do. You will learn how plants get water, keep from falling over, and protect themselves.

Did you know plants can make their own food? The next story explains how they do this.

Science is not just about discovery. You'll meet a scientist who used his discoveries to help farmers grow better crops.

Last, you will read about a scientist who studied plants. What she learned about Indian corn helped many scientists who study genetics. Why did it take so long for other scientists to accept what she found?

KENNETH M. GALE, BUGWOOD.ORG, U.S. FOREST SERVICE

Water lilies are called hydrophytes. They are freshwater plants that are found in most parts of the world. They often have large leaves and showy, colorful flowers.

It Takes TEAMWORK

Above: **Each part of a plant—root, stem, leaf, and flower—has a different job to do, but all parts of the plant work together to help the plant grow.**

JUPITERIMAGES

Left: **Every winter, syrup-makers collect sap from maple trees by drilling a hole in the tree trunk, putting a tube called a spout into the trunk, then hanging a bucket from the spout. The sap will leak through the spout and into the bucket.**

AGRICULTURAL RESEARCH SERVICE, USDA

If you play sports, you know that the best teams have players who work well together. Each team member has a role to play. It's the same with plants. Have you noticed that all plants have similar parts? Each part of a plant has a different job that helps keep the plant alive.

Roots and Stems

Let's start at the bottom of a plant—the roots. You will read more about roots later. Roots keep the plant in place and absorb water and nutrients (not food). Moving up from the roots, we see that plants have stems. Stems connect the roots to the leaves and flowers. Stems support the plant so that it doesn't droop or fall over. Stems, like roots, contain veins. The veins, like little hoses, carry sap to all parts of the plant.

What is sap? It is the gooey stuff that you will find inside plants. Sap carries water and food to and from different parts of the plant. Think of the tallest tree you've ever seen. It's a plant, too. The trunk of that tree is its main stem. That tall tree has a lot of sap to carry nutrients from its roots all the way to its highest leaf, way up in the sky.

COURTESY OF UNITED STATES DEPARTMENT OF AGRICULTURE

Pines have needle-like leaves and are evergreen, which means they have green leaves throughout the year.

JEFFREY W. LOTZ, FLORIDA DEPARTMENT OF AGRICULTURE AND CONSUMER SERVICES, BUGWOOD.ORG, U.S. FOREST SERVICE

Have you ever eaten pancakes or waffles with maple syrup? Maple syrup is made from the sap of a maple tree. Maple trees grow mainly in the eastern United States and Canada.

Leaves and Flowers

Moving along the stems of a plant we find leaves. Leaves collect energy from the sun. During the day, the sun shines brightly. Sunlight is energy. Plants use sunlight to make sugars that they use as food. Leaves have special parts that help them collect sunlight, make sugar, and send the sugar they make to other parts of the plant.

Go outside and look at a leaf. What do you notice about the leaf? The leaves of most flowering plants are thin and flat. Can you tell the difference between the top and the bottom? The top of the leaf usually faces the sun and is often shiny. The bottom of the leaf is often rough and duller. The leaf has tube-like veins that carry the sugar made in the leaf to the rest of the plant.

Leaves come in many shapes and sizes, which may depend on where a plant lives. A plant living in the shade may have bigger leaves to help it collect more sunlight. A plant living where it's sunny most of the time, such as in a desert, may have smaller, thicker leaves to save water.

And finally, at the ends of the stems are flowers. Flowers make fruits, and fruits contain seeds that can grow into new plants. Apples are fruits that come from the flower of an apple tree. Try planting seeds from the next apple you eat. Maybe you'll grow your own apple tree.

The different parts of plants help the plant make its own food, gather water and nutrients, and stand up tall. Do you have the same kinds of parts? ■

Grasses have long, narrow leaves and have been grown as a food source for domesticated animals, such as cattle, for up to 10,000 years. The cereal grasses like wheat, oats, and rice are important foods for people.

COURTESY OF UNITED STATES DEPARTMENT OF AGRICULTURE

Apples are fruits that come in many colors and sizes. What is your favorite kind of apple?

Getting to the Root of It

Have you ever looked closely at plant roots? Carefully pull a dandelion out of the ground and look at its roots. Dandelion roots are usually light colored and have many little "hairs" growing out in every direction. Why do you think they grow like this? Do you think that all plant roots look the same? Read on to find out more.

Carrots are root vegetables and are a good source of vitamin A, which is important for strong bones and healthy skin.

Taraxacum officinale **is the scientific name for the common dandelion plant shown in this drawing. Botanical drawings are used by scientists to help identify plants.**

Roots help the plant in three ways. They keep the plant in one place. They absorb the nutrients and water that the plant needs to survive and grow. Some plants even have roots that store extra food until the plant needs to use it. The roots of plants look different depending upon where the plant lives and what the plant needs to stay alive.

Not All Plants Grow out of the Ground

Some plants live in water. These plants are called hydrophytes. *Hydro* means "water" and *phyte* means "plant." One example of a hydrophyte is a water lily. You may have seen water lilies floating on top of a pond. They have big, round, flat leaves. Hydrophytes have stems under water that absorb water and nutrients, so they don't have to depend as much on their roots for water as a plant

Water lilies are called hydrophytes. They are freshwater plants that are found in most parts of the world. They often have large leaves and showy, colorful flowers.

This epiphyte, Spanish moss, is native to warm parts of America like the Southern states. Would you believe that it is not really a moss but in the same plant family as the pineapple? It's true!

COURTESY OF THE U.S. GEOLOGICAL SURVEY

that lives in soil does. Hydrophytes' roots are very small.

Epiphytes are plants that grow attached to another living thing—usually another plant. *Epi* means "upon" and *phyte* means—well, you know what phyte means! One example of an epiphyte is Spanish moss. The roots of some epiphytes are thin and threadlike so that they can grab onto other plants and stay attached. Some epiphytes use their leaves, rather than their roots, to absorb water from the air or from raindrops.

A cactus is a xerophyte (say: ZEER-uh-fight) that is common in dry areas like the desert. (*Xerophyte* means "dry plant.") Cactus plants can also live in humid places where the soil is sandy and can't easily hold water. What do you suppose the roots of a cactus look like? Because there is so little water in the desert or the soil, most cactus plants have roots that are very close to the surface of the ground. How would that help a cactus plant after a rainstorm?

You may be surprised to learn that there are a number of roots that you eat!

Remember that you read about roots that store food for the plant? These roots provide food for us as well! (You can read more about food plants on page 7.) Examples of these edible roots are sweet potatoes, radishes, and carrots. ■

COURTESY OF UNITED STATES DEPARTMENT OF AGRICULTURE

ROBERT W. FRECKMANN, UNIVERSITY OF WISCONSIN-STEVENS POINT

Like carrots, radishes are root vegetables that are used in salads and as a relish for their peppery taste.

A cactus is a unique plant that comes in many shapes and sizes. It can live in very dry and hot environments. Many cactus plants have large stems for storing water.

OUCH!
That Plant Bit Me!

Imagine that a large animal wants to eat you. What do you do? People and other animals can run away and hide. Plants can't move. How do plants keep from being eaten? It turns out that plants have different ways of protecting themselves.

Poisons and Thorns and Fuzz

Some plants make chemicals that don't harm the plant but do harm the animal that eats it. Some plants taste bad. Tasting bad doesn't hurt the plant. It can't taste itself. But animals don't want to eat a plant that tastes bad. Do you?

Other plants are poisonous. Poisons can make animals sick or kill them. If a cat eats even a tiny bit of a lily plant, it could get really sick.

Have you ever picked blackberries? Raspberries? Or roses? How are these plants alike? You're right if you guessed that the stems and leaves are covered with prickly thorns. Thorns scratch and poke your skin. They hurt! Imagine you're an animal trying to pick berries with your snout. OUCH!

The kiwifruit is named after the national bird of New Zealand, the kiwi. The flavor of the fruit is described as a mix of strawberry, banana, and pineapple, and is a rich source of vitamin C.

The pineapple is a tropical plant with spiny leaves. The pineapple fruit is very sweet and juicy.

The spines and hairs of cactus are actually leaves. The spines shade the plant from the hot sun and protect the cactus from animals.

The sensitive plant grows in the tropics. Because its leaves close and droop at the lightest touch, grasshoppers, cattle, and other herbivores don't eat it. The leaves also close when there is too much heat or too little light or water.

(BOTH) BLUEMOOSE, CREATIVE COMMONS ATTRIBUTION SHAREALIKE LICENSE VERSIONS 2.5, 2.0

JIM CONRAD, NATURALIST NEWSLETTER, WWW.BACKYARDNATURE.NET

Some fruits, like peaches and kiwis, are covered with hairs that can make your mouth itch. And pineapples have a prickly outside and hurt to bite into. How do you eat pineapple?

The sensitive plant has leaves that fold up when touched by an insect or rain or even your fingertip. If the insects can't stay on the leaf, they can't eat it!

You Scratch My Back . . .

Other plants use more complicated ways to protect themselves. Bullhorn acacia trees, for example, have large hollow spines on their trunks. Ants hide in these spines to keep from being eaten. They protect the tree from other animals by stinging anything that touches it. The ants also remove the seedlings, or young plants, of other plants that try to grow under the acacia tree. In turn, the tree makes nectar and food that the ants can eat. The ants and the tree protect each other. This type of relationship, where two different living beings help each other, is called mutualism.

Thousands of ants can live in one bullhorn acacia tree with their nests in the thorns.

Plants can't run away from danger, but they can protect themselves in many other ways. Some taste bad, some have thorns, and some use insects such as ants to help them. Can you think of other ways plants protect themselves? ■

Making Food out of AIR

Chlorophyll is a chemical in plants that makes leaves and stems green. Chlorophyll is important in plant photosynthesis.

What did you eat for dinner last night? If you ate vegetables, you ate plants. If you ate chicken, in a way you ate plants, too. Why? What do chickens eat? Chickens eat seeds, and seeds come from plants.

All animals, including people, depend on plants for food. Plants can make their own food using air and water, and we can't. If you can't find any food to eat and can't make your own, you could be very hungry!

Plants Are Producers

How do plants make their own food? In another story you read that plants collect energy from the sun. Do you remember what part of a plant collects sunlight? Plants use sunlight to make their own food, a kind of sugar.

Plants make sugar through photosynthesis, (say: fo-to-SIN-the-sis). *Photo* means "light" and *synthesis* means "to make." Photosynthesis means using light to make food. Plants are called producers because they make food.

What special things do plants need for photosynthesis? To answer this question, it is helpful to think about what plants look like.

Most plants are green. The green in plants comes from a chemical found in leaves and stems. The chemical, chlorophyll, (say: CLOR-oh-fill), captures sunlight that plants use to make food.

What else do plants need for photosynthesis? Think of what a plant needs to stay alive. What happens if you forget to water a plant? Or leave it in the dark? Plants need sunlight and water for photosynthesis. You already learned how a plant collects sunlight with its leaves.

LIGHT ENERGY

OXYGEN

CARBON DIOXIDE

WATER

NSRC

Nearly all life on Earth depends on plant photosynthesis. This diagram shows the pathways of sunlight, water, and air in this process.

What Is Carbon Dioxide?

Carbon dioxide is found in air. It has no color, taste, or smell. Animals and people breathe in oxygen and breathe out carbon dioxide. Other things make carbon dioxide. Cars, buses, and trucks make it from burning gasoline. Burning a fire in your fireplace or at a campsite or in a barbecue makes carbon dioxide. So do volcanoes. Factories and power plants also make it. Have you ever seen smoke coming from a factory? That smoke contains carbon dioxide. Today there is a lot more carbon dioxide in our air than there was just a few years ago. Scientists are studying the question of what may happen with the extra carbon dioxide in our environment.

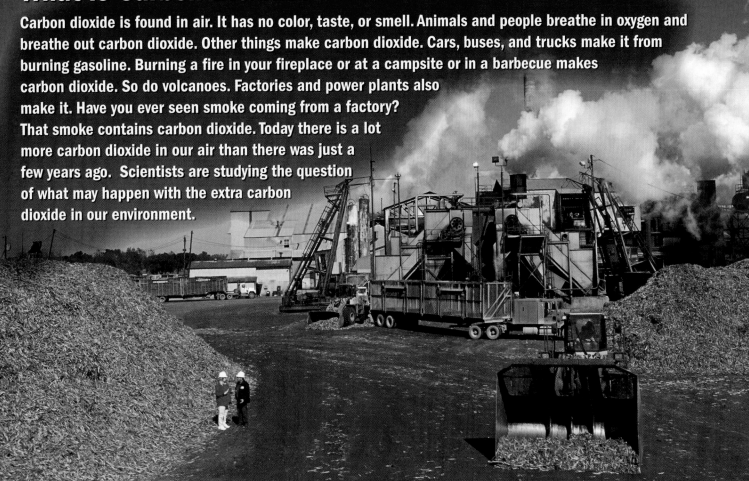

COURTESY OF UNITED STATES DEPARTMENT OF AGRICULTURE

© IMAGES & STORIES/ALAMY

How does a plant get water? Their roots—and in some plants their leaves or stems—collect water. The water can also carry important nutrients that plants need to grow.

One last substance that plants need for photosynthesis is in the air. Air is a mixture of different substances. For example, air contains oxygen and carbon dioxide. During photosynthesis plants use part of the air to make food. The part of the air they use is carbon dioxide.

When Does Photosynthesis Take Place?

You know that plants need sunlight to grow. During the day, plant leaves capture sunlight energy. This energy changes carbon dioxide from the air and water from the roots into a sugar. ▶

Kelp forests are really giant seaweeds. They grow in cool coastal waters where sunlight can reach a rocky ocean floor. These giant seaweeds also depend on sunlight for photosynthesis.

Some of the sugar is sent to the seeds, roots, and stems, where it is stored and used as food. It is this food that keeps the plant alive, and us alive too.

Plants are important to life on Earth. They produce food for themselves and other living things. Plants also use carbon dioxide and release oxygen into the air. This is good for animals because they need oxygen to live. ■

You will stop growing taller when you're older, no matter how much you eat.

Do plants stop growing? Bert Drake says the answer is no—some plants will keep growing if they have enough carbon dioxide and water.

Bert is a scientist at the Smithsonian Environmental Research Center in Maryland. He has studied the growth of marsh plants for 20 years. Marsh plants are special plants that grow in shallow water and soggy soil.

(BOTH) KIMBRA CUTLIP, SMITHSONIAN ENVIRONMENTAL RESEARCH CENTER

One of Bert's experiments was to give marsh plants more carbon dioxide to see if they would keep growing. But carbon dioxide is part of the air. It just floats away! What did Bert do? He built clear plastic houses around the plants and added carbon dioxide to the houses.

The Smithsonian Environmental Research Center's carbon dioxide chambers glow in the night.

For many years, Bert measured the plants in the houses. He compared them to plants outside the houses. Some plants were the same size. But other plants grew bigger inside the houses. They kept growing and growing!

Today, there is more carbon dioxide in the air than there was 20 years ago. What do you think will happen to all the plants on Earth? Bert knows that with more carbon dioxide, some plants will grow faster than other plants. How do you think this could change our world?

Scientist Bert Drake sits next to a carbon dioxide chamber.

George Washington Carver lived from about 1864 to 1943.

A Farmer's Friend

GEORGE WASHINGTON CARVER liked to dig in the dirt and he loved plants.
As a child, he looked for plants when he walked in the woods and
studied them in his garden. If he found a sick plant, he nursed it.
People called him "The Plant Doctor."
Carver grew up to become a famous scientist. He taught at Tuskegee Institute (now
Tuskegee University) in Alabama, one of the nation's first colleges for African
Americans. He helped farmers raise healthy plants and he was an inventor. But most
of all he is remembered as a person who cared for the land and farmers. ▷

Be Kind to Your Fellow Man and the Soil

Carver was born a slave during the Civil War. He lost his father and his mother when he was very young. Growing up, he learned the importance of kindness, and was grateful when he got help. Although slavery ended after the Civil War, it was especially hard for a young African American man to get an education in the 1800s in the United States. But he didn't give up, and he graduated from college. Carver wanted to use his education to help poor African American farmers. The first thing he told them was, "Be kind to the soil." Read on to see what he meant by that.

King Cotton Robs the Soil

Carver saw that many farmers in Alabama were not being smart. They grew cotton every year. "King Cotton" made a lot of money for them. But the good times didn't last. After a few years of growing cotton, the soil lost nutrients. Then the cotton did not grow well, and the farmers had to move to new fields.

But many southern farmers didn't have a lot of land. They planted in the same fields year after year, making less and less money. Carver knew it didn't have to be that way. He taught farmers how to take care of the soil and make a good living. His plan was called crop rotation.

Giving Back to the Soil

Some crops use up nutrients as they grow, but others add nutrients to the soil. Carver told farmers to plant a different crop on a field each year. After each crop that took nutrients from the soil, they should plant a crop that gave nutrients back. After cotton, farmers should plant peanuts or soybeans. After corn or tomatoes or lettuce, they could plant sweet potatoes. With crop rotation, the soil gained nutrients. The crops were good, and farmers were able to make a good living.

Farmers can divide a field into sections and put different plants in each section. Cotton, corn, and tomatoes use the nutrients in the soil. Peanuts, soybeans, and sweet potatoes put them back.

YEAR 1

A	B
COTTON	SWEET POTATOES
D	C
SOYBEANS AND PEANUTS	CORN AND TOMATOES

YEAR 2

A	B
SOYBEANS AND PEANUTS	COTTON
D	C
CORN AND TOMATOES	SWEET POTATOES

Inventing New Products

Carver had talked farmers into growing peanuts, soybeans, and sweet potatoes. Now he wanted to find new uses for these crops, so farmers could sell them easily. He became an inventor and found about 300 ways to use peanuts. He used peanuts and sweet potatoes to make paper, dyes, fuel, glue, hand cream, and other useful products. And he became a great cook! I bet you've had his most famous recipe for lunch once or twice. It goes on bread along with jelly. You guessed it—peanut butter.

Carver is admired by many Americans, not just farmers. We are grateful for his ideas about crop rotation, and for all his discoveries about plants and soil. But his kindness made him a remarkable man. ■

NATIONAL PARK SERVICE

COURTESY OF UNITED STATES DEPARTMENT OF AGRICULTURE

Above: "He could have added fortune to fame, but caring for neither, he found happiness and honor in being helpful to the world." —On the gravestone of George Washington Carver.

Left: Carver discovered 300 uses for peanuts. This picture shows peanuts in the shell. What is your favorite way to eat peanuts?

CORN AND TOMATOES

SOYBEANS AND PEANUTS

SWEET POTATOES

COTTON

YEAR 3

SWEET POTATOES

CORN AND TOMATOES

COTTON

SOYBEANS AND PEANUTS

YEAR 4

A Scientist Who Wouldn't Give Up

Barbara McClintock (1902-1992) studies corn in her lab.

Do you look like your parents? Like your grandparents? Why do you look like your mom, while your brother looks like your dad? The answer is genetics. Genetics is the science of how parents pass on traits, like eye and hair color, to their children. Geneticists are scientists who study genes, bits of information in your body that give you your traits.

Look at the picture of this family. Can you see how traits like hair and eye color are shared by some members of the family?

Blue Eyes and Red Roses

It's not just people who have traits. Plants have traits, too—color and size, for example. Roses come in all sorts of colors: red, yellow, pink, white, and even black! Tomatoes come in red, orange, and yellow. Some are as large as softballs, and some are as small as grapes. Barbara McClintock wondered if plants pass on traits the same way that people do.

Indian Corn

When she was in school, McClintock liked science class. That's where she learned about genetics. She was a student at Cornell University in the 1920s. Can you figure out how long ago that was? Genetics was a new science then. People didn't know very much about it. But McClintock liked genetics so much that she spent the rest of her life studying it.

McClintock studied Indian corn, the corn you see around Thanksgiving. What does Indian corn look like? Indian corn has many different colors. Color is one kind of trait. Most of the corn on the cob we eat is all yellow or all white, or a mix of yellow and white. But Indian corn can be black, blue, red, white, or yellow. Many ears of Indian corn have kernels of more than one color! McClintock wondered how one ear could have many different colors.

McClintock spent years planting corn and looking at the colors of the new corn. She planted kernels of different colors. When the little plants grew up to grow their own ears of corn, she looked at the colors. Did an orange kernel make an all-orange ear of corn? Did a blue kernel make an all-blue ear of corn? No—the ears were mixed colors again! How did this happen?

After many experiments, she came to one explanation about how these changes happened in Indian corn. It was because something was happening to the genes that cause the color traits. The genes must be moving around in the growing corn. Each time the gene jumped, it changed the color of the kernel!

Disbelief

In the 1950s, McClintock told other scientists what she thought was making Indian corn different colors. But few believed her. Some scientists got mad at her because they thought her idea of "jumping genes" was ridiculous. Even though people didn't believe her, she didn't give up. She continued to study corn.

As time passed, scientific tools got better. Soon, other scientists saw that McClintock had been right all along. She had made an ▶

COURTESY OF UNITED STATES DEPARTMENT OF AGRICULTURE

Corn comes in many colors, and McClintock was interested in the many colors of Indian corn.

PAPA GENO'S HERB FARM

Tomatoes are grown around the world and come in many sizes and colors.

about diseases that can be passed on from parents to children in genes. Sometimes, it is a "jumping gene" that can make a disease begin or not.

Awards

In 1944, McClintock became the third woman elected to the National Academy of Sciences. In 1970, she was awarded the National Medal of Science for her discovery. This prize is the highest award in science in the United States. In 1983, she won another great award called the Nobel Prize. She was the first American woman to win a Nobel Prize in Medicine by herself. But to McClintock, the awards were less important than the scientific discovery.

McClintock continued to study corn until her death in 1992. It's a good thing she never gave up her ideas. ■

important discovery that genes can move around. What she had discovered in corn was true for other plants and animals, too.

Her discoveries helped scientists learn how traits can be turned on and off. The "jumping gene" can act like a light switch that can turn on and off the genes that follow it. This discovery is still very important today as scientists do research

NATIONAL SCIENCE AND TECHNOLOGY MEDALS FOUNDATION

In 1970, McClintock received her National Medal of Science from President Richard M. Nixon.

CONCLUSION PART 2

Plants Are Amazing!

THAT'S A FACT!

Maple syrup that tastes so good on pancakes comes from the sap of the maple tree. Maple trees grow mainly in the northeastern part of the United States and Canada.

I KNOW THAT!

What is the difference between an epiphyte and a hydrophyte?

WHAT DO YOU THINK?

What do plants need to make their own food by photosynthesis?

HERE'S ONE MORE!

Why did George Washington Carver tell farmers to use crop rotation?

PART 3

Plants and Animals Living Together

The stories in this section will show you some of the surprising ways in which plants and animals interact with each other. They are:

- **Making New Plants**
- **On the Road with Beekeepers**
- **Desert Survivors**
- **Achoo!**
- **Lions and Zebras and Chimps, Oh My!**

In the first story you will learn about the importance of plant pollination. You'll discover hardworking bees and tricky orchids.

Then you'll meet a beekeeper and learn about his trade. Thanks to beekeepers, there are more fruits and vegetables on your table.

Not just people depend on plants for food. You'll read about the favorite foods of desert tortoises and how these tortoises can survive without water for long periods of time.

Next, you'll see how the pollination cycle of plants can affect even you!

And finally you'll find that each plant and each animal has its very own place in the circle of life. Take a look. Can you decide where your place might be?

COURTESY OF UNITED STATES DEPARTMENT OF AGRICULTURE

Whenever beekeepers are working with bees, they have to wear special clothes that protect them from stings. They also wear a hat with a veil.

Making New Plants

HAVE YOU EVER WONDERED WHY PLANTS HAVE FLOWERS? WHILE MOST FLOWERS ARE PRETTY, THEY'RE NOT JUST FOR LOOKS. THE MAIN PURPOSE OF FLOWERS IS TO ATTRACT POLLINATORS. WHO ARE THESE POLLINATORS, AND WHY ARE THEY SO IMPORTANT TO PLANTS?

COURTESY OF UNITED STATES DEPARTMENT OF AGRICULTURE

STIGMA

ANTHER

The anther is the part of the flower where the pollen is produced, and the stigma is the part that can receive pollen during pollination.

This honeybee has pollen sticking to the hairs under its body. When the bee visits a flower, the pollen could fall down onto the flower's stigma.

COURTESY OF U.S. FOREST SERVICE

Pollinators can be as small as an insect or as big as a bird. Pollinators such as bees, butterflies, hummingbirds, and bats have at least one thing in common. They move pollen around the flower or from flower to flower. This must happen before a plant can produce seeds and new plants. ▶

Flower Power

Let's look closely at a flower. Pollen is a powder that is made in the part of a flower called the anther. Pollen needs to move from the anther to another part of the flower called the stigma. This process is called pollination. If pollen reaches the stigma, it may fertilize the flower. When the flower dies, a fruit with one or more seeds begins to grow in its place, and these seeds may grow into a new plant.

Since most plants are rooted in the ground, they need help with this process of pollination. For some plants, the wind carries pollen to other flowers and plants. Others need pollinators, like the bees and

MAEK WHITTEN, FLORIDA MUSEUM OF NATURAL HISTORY, UNIVERSITY OF FLORIDA

Packets of orchid pollen, called pollinia, stick to the body of this insect and could be carried away by the insect to pollinate another flower.

hummingbirds that you read about on page 39.

The bright colors and sweet smells of flowers attract pollinators. The pollinators, in turn, get food—pollen and nectar—from the plants. When insects and other animals gather nectar and

Darwin's Prediction

WIKIPEDIA COMMONS

Long ago scientists described mutualism between plants and animals in pollination. In England, the famous naturalist Charles Darwin studied a white flower that came from the island of Madagascar. The nectar was at the end of a long tube. It bloomed only at night. Although he never saw the insect, Darwin thought that the pollinator must be a moth with a really long tongue. Moths fly at night. They are able to see white flowers at night. The pollinator would need a long tongue to reach the nectar. Thirty years after Darwin's prediction, the moth was found!

COURTESY OF TONY WATKINSON

pollen from flowers, some pollen may stick to their body. As these pollinators move around the flower, or from flower to flower, they can move pollen from the anther to the sticky stigma, and complete the pollination process.

In the end, both the plant and the pollinator gain something. The plant is pollinated and able to produce seeds that may grow into new plants. The pollinators gather food for themselves and their offspring. Scientists call this mutualism when two living organisms interact and both of them benefit. ■

With its long tongue, this moth is able to reach the nectar from the white Madagascar flower studied by Darwin.

Not All Orchids Are What They Seem

Orchids have many ways to attract the right pollinators, so that little packets of pollen get stuck to their bodies. The packets, called pollinia, are then carried by the pollinator to another flower. But some orchids are tricky; they don't give the pollinator what they seem to offer. The orchid *Ophrys* has flowers that look like female bees or wasps. Males try to mate with the orchid. By the time they realize the flower is not another bee or wasp, they've picked up sticky pollinia on their body to carry to another flower for pollination.

Another orchid, *Coryanthes*, has a wide lip like a bucket that is full of a sticky liquid. When insects come to the orchid's sweet smell, they fall in the "bucket" and start to drown. One way out is through a tube where the pollen packets, pollinia, are located. If the insect is too small, the pollinia won't stick. If the insect is too large, it can't fit in the tube and may drown if it can't find another way out. Only the right-sized insect passes pollen on to another orchid.

COURTESY OF MANFRED AYASSE, UNIVERSITY OF ULM, GERMANY

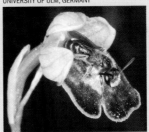

This *Ophrys* orchid attracts male bees because it looks like a female. With a little luck, pollen will be moved by the bee to another *Ophrys* orchid.

COURTESY OF DR. GUNTER GERLACH, BOTANISCHER GARTEN MÜNCHEN-NYMPHENBURG

This bee has yellow pollinia on its back after climbing out of the sticky trap of the *Coryanthes* orchid. Now the bee could carry the pollen to another *Coryanthes* orchid.

On the Road with Beekeepers

COURTESY OF TESS ARNOLD

Beekeeper Tess Arnold takes care of his beehives and provides a pollination service to farmers.

Think of a field of pumpkins. Bees pollinate the pumpkin flowers, which grow into large, orange pumpkins. The farmer wants to grow as many pumpkins as he can, and to get more pumpkins you need more bees. Who will the farmer call? The beekeeper!

A beekeeper will bring a colony of honeybees for each acre in the pumpkin field. A colony has a queen bee and thousands of worker bees, often in a large wooden box. The farmer can get twice as many pumpkins when an extra bee colony is around. More fruit means more money for the farmer and his family.

On the Road Again!

Beekeepers move their colonies from field to field. Tess Arnold takes his colonies to Florida in November. The weather is warm in Florida, and many, many bees are born. By late February, there may be 30,000 to 40,000 bees in each colony. Tess puts screens on the hives and puts them in a tractor-trailer truck. He takes his bees to orange and lemon groves. His bees pollinate the orange and lemon flowers.

In a few weeks, all the orange and lemon trees are finished blooming.

TETRA IMAGES/ALAMY

Honeybees are important pollinators for pumpkin plants, producing fields of fat, orange pumpkins. The insides of pumpkins are a popular food, and many pumpkins also become jack-o'-lanterns at Halloween.

Whenever beekeepers are working with bees, they have to wear special clothes that protect them from stings. They also wear a hat with a veil.

COURTESY OF UNITED STATES DEPARTMENT OF AGRICULTURE

More than Pollination

Remember, bees don't set out to pollinate flowers. They're gathering food to take back to their hive. They collect nectar and pollen from flowers to make honey and beebread for the colony. A bee may visit hundreds of flowers in a single trip away from the colony. During those visits, the bees pollinate while they do their job.

Beekeepers take care of the hives. They provide pollination services to farmers. And they can also harvest the honey in the hives to sell.

It is good that we have bees and beekeepers. We have more fruits and vegetables. And we have honey. Sweet! ■

He puts the screens back on the hives, loads them back in the truck, and heads north. Next are the peach orchards in Georgia, and then, apple orchards in Virginia. Finally he's off to New England, where apples and other fruit trees are just coming into bloom. Once the fruit trees are pollinated, he goes farther north to Maine to pollinate the blueberry fields and cranberry bogs. By the time Tess is done, he may not have as many bees as when he started. He goes back to Florida and lets his colonies grow again.

Right: The queen bee, shown in the middle of this photo, is the only female in the hive that lays eggs. The worker bees are females too, but they search for food and take care of the young bees and the hive.

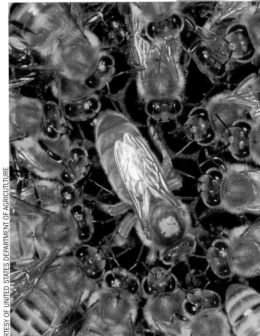

COURTESY OF UNITED STATES DEPARTMENT OF AGRICULTURE

Left: Tess Arnold holds a honeycomb that bees have filled with honey. A colony of bees eats more than 100 pounds of honey in one year. But they make a lot more. Beekeepers can remove some of the honey and sell it.

COURTESY OF TESS ARNOLD

Desert Survivors

The desert tortoise has a hard shell around its body and scales on its legs for protection. This old male lives in the Mojave Desert.

I f your favorite food isn't on the menu, you won't starve. You'll choose something else. If your favorite restaurant is closed, you won't go hungry. You'll go to a different restaurant, even one you don't like as much. Or you'll go back home and have a peanut butter and jelly sandwich.

Animals have to be flexible just like you do. If they can't find their favorite food, they have to choose another. If there is no food at all, they have to get by without food, until there is some. Read on and you'll learn how the amazing desert tortoise can survive with little or no food or water.

Life in the Slow Lane

The desert tortoise is a land turtle, and lives in the deserts of California, Arizona, Nevada, and Utah. It is a herbivore, which means that it eats plants. Its favorite foods are desert lupine, desert dandelion, and deer vetch. These are plants that have the protein the tortoise likes and needs.

But life in the desert is uncertain. Some years there can be big rainstorms, and there are plenty of lupines, dandelions, and vetch. The tortoise eats and eats and eats, storing food in its body.

NATIONAL PARK SERVICE

The Mojave Desert occupies a large part of southern California as well as small parts of Utah, Nevada, and Arizona. This vast area usually receives less than 6 inches (150 mm) of rain each year.

COURTESY OF KEN NAGY

This baby desert tortoise is able to survive in areas where the ground temperature can be higher than 140 degrees Fahrenheit (60 degrees Celsius). It digs underground burrows and escapes the heat.

But then there are dry years, and it may rain just a little or not at all. Lupines, dandelions, and vetch don't grow well if there is not enough rain. The tortoise has to eat plants that aren't quite so tasty and don't have as much protein.

When it doesn't rain at all, the tortoise may have nothing to eat or drink, and must use a special adaptation to survive. The tortoise goes down to its underground burrow and waits until it rains again. It may stay there for as long as a year and a half! How can it do this? A Smithsonian scientist, Olav Oftedal, working with other scientists, discovered some interesting facts.

In the good times when the rains and plants come, the tortoise may leave its burrow every night. When it returns to the burrow, it can slow some body processes like breathing and digesting, and save energy.

During the dry times, when there is no water at all, the tortoise can stay in its cool burrow for a long time. It slows down its body processes a lot and waits for the rains to come. Look at the Desert Tortoise Information table on this page.

The Desert Tortoise: Master Recycler

But the most amazing adaptation is what the tortoise's body does with its waste. Most animals get rid of their poisonous waste products in urine. When the tortoise is active, it does the same. But when it is burrowed into the ground for more than a year, it has another adaptation. It uses the protein it has eaten to pull the poisons out of its urine. The poisons are made into little pellets. After its body expels the little pellets, the tortoise reuses the clean water left inside its bladder. Now that's recycling to the max! ■

Desert Tortoise Information

DESCRIPTION	WET YEAR	DRY YEAR
Rainfall in a year	34 to 310 mm	0 mm
Percent of tortoises active during a typical day	55%	18%
Heart rate	30 beats per minute (active with a warm body)	1 beat every 2 minutes (in burrow with a cool body)
Breathing rate	8 breaths each minute (active)	1 breath each 5 minutes (in burrow)

What does this information tell us about how a tortoise can survive?

ACHOO!

Do you have a frog in your throat? A sneeze in your head? A runny nose? An itch in your eye? You may think you have a nasty cold. But maybe you got caught in the pollination cycle of a plant and your body doesn't like it!

You may have an allergy to pollen. Some people call allergies hay fever. But there is no fever. And allergies are caused by many plants.

Swirling Clouds of Pollen

Trees, grasses, and weeds send pollen into the air. Pollen is a part of a plant that helps it to reproduce. The tiny pollen grains can travel for miles. They hitch a ride in the wind. They mix into the air we breathe. Some folks breathe pollen-filled air with no problem. Others have allergies.

JON SULLIVAN, PDPHOTO.ORG

This showy flower has sticky, yellow pollen and attracts insects. But if you put your nose too close, you could breathe in some pollen.

The Fighting Armies

Your immune system is your body's fix-it shop. It has an army of cells ready to take care of trouble. When you skin your knee or have a tummy ache, these cells fix the problem. Bacteria and viruses are tiny organisms that can cause disease. When they enter your body, immune system armies work to destroy them. When we breathe in something harmless,

DARTMOUTH ELECTRON MICROSCOPE FACILITY, DARTMOUTH COLLEGE

These tiny pollen grains are magnified 500 times. They can ride for miles on the wind. Some pollen can fall on other flowers, and some may be in the air you breathe.

like pollen, the immune systems should not go to work. Most people breathe in pollen and channel it through the nose and mouth into their stomachs. They don't even notice the pollen!

Too Much!

If you are someone who has allergies, then you have a sensitive immune system. You could say that your body reacts too much. When your system reacts to pollen, we say you have an allergic reaction to pollen. Your immune system releases fighting cells and chemicals when it detects pollen in your airways. One chemical that causes problems is histamine. Too much histamine ends up in your nose, throat, or eyes, trying to fight the harmless enemy. It can cause changes in your body that give you the itchy eyes, runny nose, and itchy throat. So, it's really not the pollen that is the problem, but your body's reaction to pollen that is causing you problems.

Some people take allergy shots of a tiny amount of pollen, so their bodies will learn to not treat pollen as an enemy.

Your Battle Plan

It happens like clockwork. Different trees, grasses, and weeds go through pollination cycles at the same time each year in the spring, summer, and fall. But don't worry. Doctors and scientists have found ways to stop or relieve many allergic reactions. First, you can avoid breathing so much pollen by staying indoors on "high pollen days." You can take medications, like antihistamines, that ease your allergic reaction to pollen. And finally, your doctor may give you allergy shots that may help you react less to the pollen. You can fight back. ■

Ragweed plants like this are probably to blame if you have allergies in the fall. If you have the sneezes in the spring, you may be allergic to tree pollen. If you have allergies in the summer, grass pollen could be your problem.

STEVE DEWEY, UTAH STATE UNIVERSITY, BUGWOOD.ORG, USDA FOREST SERVICE

© CHARLES GULLUNG/ZEFA/CORBIS.COM

Lions and Zebras and Chimps, Oh My!

Does a mighty lion depend on a tiny plant? Oh, yes! Lions may not actually eat plants, but they do eat many animals that eat plants. They eat gazelles and zebras and other animals that graze on the African plains. Without plants, lions would be quite hungry. They don't eat plants; but they definitely depend on them.

Herbivores, Carnivores, and Omnivores

Many animals eat plants. We call them herbivores. Cows, deer, and giraffes are all herbivores.

Some animals, like tigers, eat the meat of other animals. We call them carnivores. They eat the meat of animals that eat plants or other animals.

Some animals eat both plants and other animals. We call them omnivores. You're probably sitting in a classroom full of omnivores, since many people eat both plants and animal products.

Like many of us, the chimpanzee is an omnivore. Chimpanzees are known to eat both plants and animals.

Zebras are white with black stripes. Each zebra's stripes are a little different. Many scientists believe the stripes help the zebra hide on the grassy plains of Africa from their main predator, the lion. The lion is colorblind.

Lions often hunt in groups. They can bring down large animals, such as antelopes, buffalos, and zebras.

Animals need plants because they cannot make their own food. Animals are consumers; they use food. Plants are producers; they make food. Plants take the energy of the sun, carbon dioxide from the air, and water and minerals from the soil to make their food. You can read the story on page 28 about plants and photosynthesis to find out more about this process.

The Food Chain

A food chain is another way to look at producers and consumers. Food chains show how energy from plant producers reaches animal consumers. Look at the food chain to the right. A beetle feeds on plants. A robin eats the beetle. A hawk eats the robin. The hawk is the last consumer on the food chain. The beetle, the robin, and the hawk all depend on plants, the producers.

It's Not Just a Chain

The interaction between plants and animals can be very complicated and often not as simple as a food chain. Scientists like to look at ecosystems, or communities of plants and animals that live together in a particular place. They use a food web, like the one below, to describe these communities. ▶

This food chain shows a simple path of energy flowing from one organism to the next. It also shows how energy from plant producers reaches animal consumers.

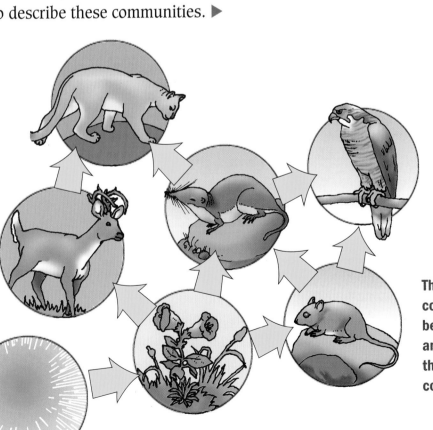

The food web shows how complicated the links are between the plant producers and animal consumers. Follow the arrows to find out what is consuming what.

The head of the arrow points toward the animal that is being fed. In a forest you can find animals like deer and mice that eat many different plants. You may also find weasels that eat mice. In the summer, a weasel may also eat fruits and berries. Finally there are mountain lions and hawks that can feed on deer, weasels and mice. It's a jumble out there. Using food webs makes the jumble easier to understand. Did you figure out the food web puzzle?

GIL WOJCIECH, POLISH RESEARCH INSTITUTE, BUGWOOD.ORG, USDA FOREST SERVICE

Decomposers like mushrooms break down dead plants and animals. The nutrients that are left return to the soil where they can be used by plants.

Decomposers: Nature's Recyclers

One type of organism that's important to a food web is a decomposer. When a plant or animal dies, decomposers break down what's left. Sometimes you can see them. Mushrooms are decomposers and belong to group of organisms known as fungi. You can find mushrooms and other fungi growing and feeding on dead trees and leaves. Bacteria are decomposers, too. But you can only see them with a microscope since they are so small.

Decomposers free nutrients left in dead plants and animals. The nutrients return to the soil. Then plants can use the nutrients to make food during photosynthesis. Every organism depends on decomposers. They are the last link in the food chain. The circle of life continues. ■

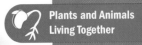
CONCLUSION PART 3

Plants and Animals Living Together

THAT'S A FACT!

Pollinators and plants often have special ways that they interact. When they both gain something, this is a kind of mutualism.

I KNOW THAT!

How do bees and beekeepers help farmers and their crops?

WHAT DO YOU THINK?

How does the desert tortoise survive when there is no rainfall and little food?

HERE'S ONE MORE!

Can you draw a food chain using wild animals and plants found in your state?

PART 4

Plants in Danger

With all living things depending on plants, it is important that we care for and protect the plant life on Earth. The stories in this section are:

- Saving Plants for Tomorrow
- Where the Tall Grass Grows
- Covered in Kudzu
- Weed Warriors Battle Plant Invaders

Did you know that some plants and ecosystems are in danger of disappearing? The first story will show you beautiful grasslands that once covered much of the center of the United States. Today, these grasslands or prairies survive only in small, protected pockets.

Next let's meet and try to defeat plant invaders. These plants threaten our native plants, and some people are trying hard to defend against the attack.

Finally, you can visit some special places that exist only to preserve and protect endangered plants. How do botanical gardens protect plants? And why should we care?

THE NATURE CONSERVANCY R.H. WIEGAND

The *Baptisia australis* or blue wild indigo plant can be used as an antiseptic and is said to keep away flies when grown near farm animals. These plants are being protected by the Weed Warriors of The Nature Conservancy.

Saving Plants for *Tomorrow*

Did you ever lose a favorite toy? Maybe you didn't keep it in a safe place. It hurts when we lose something we care about, especially if it is rare or one of a kind. Once something rare is gone, you may never find another.

When you hear the words rare, endangered, or extinct, you probably think about animals like the blue whale or the dodo bird. But plants can be endangered too! And just as zoos are important in protecting endangered animals, there are botanical gardens and conservatories that protect plants that are about to disappear.

Sheltering Endangered Plants

Many of America's most endangered plants, the ones that may become extinct if not protected, have become part of the National Collection of Endangered Plants. They are kept in different greenhouses and gardens across the United States, where they are watched and cared for. Their seeds are collected and saved. And, in time, it is hoped that their numbers will increase.

All the plants in this collection are native. This means they grew in the United States long before any people settled here. The National Collection of Endangered Plants has more than 600 native plants. It is the largest living collection of rare plants in the world! Let's look at two plants in this collection. ▶

Dr. Kathryn Kennedy is the Executive Director of the Center for Plant Conservation at the Missouri Botanical Garden in St. Louis, Missouri.

MIKE REDMER ©

The eastern prairie fringed orchid is native to tallgrass prairie in North America. It can grow up to three feet (91 cm) tall.

KATHRYN KENNEDY, MISSOURI BOTANICAL GARDEN, ST. LOUIS

Eastern Prairie Fringed Orchid

Many plants are part of the collection because their habitat is threatened. That's the case with the eastern prairie fringed orchid, which once was plentiful on tallgrass prairies. As the prairies disappeared, so did these beautiful, white flowers. (On page 56, you can find out what happened to America's prairies and where you can still go to see those tall grasses.) Today, many of the orchids are found in small patches of 50 or fewer plants. In the past, you could find thousands of eastern prairie fringed orchids in tallgrass prairies. What a wonderful sight that must have been!

Texas Wild-Rice

Another plant in the National Collection of Endangered Plants is Texas wild-rice. Rice is the edible seed of a type of grass that grows in water. Texas wild-rice grows only in the San Marcos River in central Texas. Unfortunately, the San Marcos River is getting lower and lower because industries and farms have been using more and more of the water that feeds the river. As the water level in the river goes down, the wild-rice can't survive.

It's important that we don't lose Texas wild-rice, because it has several traits that other types of rice don't have. First, it is high in lysine (say: LIE-seen), an important nutrient for people. It is also better able to fight off a disease that infects

(BOTH) TEXAS PARKS AND WILDLIFE

Texas wild-rice is only found in a small area along the San Marcos River in central Texas.

Because wild-rice is high in nutrients and has a special flavor, it has become a popular whole grain.

other kinds of rice. Finally, Texas wild-rice drops its seeds all at one time. This makes it easier to harvest.

Saving Species

Thankfully, people are working to boost the populations of Texas wild-rice, the eastern prairie fringed orchid, and the hundreds of other plants that are part of the National Collection of Endangered Plants.

"Most of the species in our collection can be saved," says Dr. Kathryn Kennedy, who oversees the project from the headquarters at the Missouri Botanical Garden in St. Louis. "But they'll be saved only if scientists and concerned citizens protect and care

Wolves are listed as endangered or threatened in the United States, because of hunting and the loss of their home range.

for them," she adds. And that's important because once something rare is gone, you may never find another. ■

Why Save Endangered Species?

Some extinctions occur naturally. But species are becoming extinct faster than ever—mostly because of people. Why should you care?

■ Many plants and animals live together and depend on each other. The loss of one living thing from an area can affect many other plants and animals. When wolves were driven from Yellowstone Park, for example, more elk survived to eat the trees that grew along streams. There were fewer trout in the streams because the trees no longer shaded the streams and kept them cool. No wolves...more elk...fewer trees... less trout.

■ Some species are important in medicine. The antibiotic penicillin was developed from a fungus.

■ Other species are important because they warn us about environmental problems. Damage to the eastern white pine warned us about increased air pollution.

Can you think of other reasons to protect endangered species?

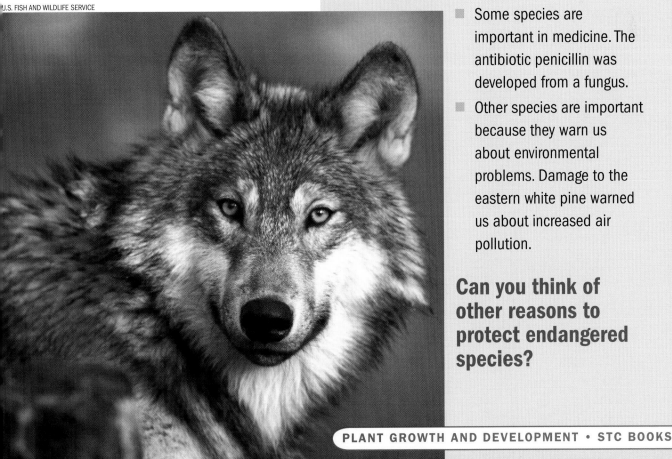

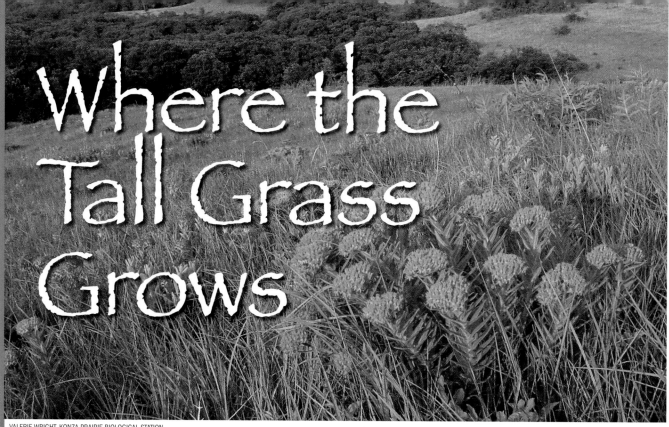

Where the Tall Grass Grows

VALERIE WRIGHT, KONZA PRAIRIE BIOLOGICAL STATION

Can you find a plant as tall as your chin growing near your home or school? If you can, stand next to it. If you can't find such a plant, simply close your eyes and pretend. Now, imagine that the plant is a bunch of grass. Imagine a sea of chin-high grasses, stretching as far as you can see. Use your mind's eye to look right and left, front and back. In all directions, the plants go on and on.

From Texas to Canada

The landscape that you are imagining really did exist and is called prairie. Tall grass, mixed grass, and short grass prairies once stretched from Texas all the way to Canada, covering much of the central United States.

Prairie grasses are not the kind of grass that people grow in their yards. After growing all spring and summer, prairie grasses often stood as tall as your chin in the low bottomlands. Some even reached twice that high! Some of these tall grasses had pale blue stems. Others were reddish. Some had large feathery plumes on top. They waved in the wind that often blew across this wide-open space.

The tallgrass prairie ecosystem is native to central North America. This is an important ecosystem because it has so many different plants and is home to so many animals.

NATIONAL PARK SERVICE

ROCK SPRINGS NATURE CENTER, O'FALLON, ILLINOIS, 2006. ROBERT LAWTON. CREATIVE COMMONS ATTRIBUTION SHAREALIKE 2.5

Huge herds of buffalo once grazed on the prairie, and pioneers built their houses on it. Over time, much of the prairie was plowed to make room for wheat, corn, and other crops needed to feed a growing nation. But in Kansas, a part of the prairie still exists. The Tallgrass Prairie National Preserve is the largest protected prairie land left on Earth. It covers an area six miles long and three miles wide.

Climate Shaped the Prairie

As big as it is, the Tallgrass Prairie National Preserve is just a miniature of what much of the country once looked like. The prairie has more rain than deserts in parts of the West. And some parts of the prairie are not wet enough for forests to grow, like they do in the East. It has dry, hot summers and cold winters—just right for grasses. And it's just right for buffalo, deer, elk, badgers, raccoons, fox, coyotes, rabbits, eagles, and many other animals.

At the Tallgrass Prairie National Preserve, you can still spot many of these animals. You can walk among the pale blue grasses. In the fall, you can watch the tall, waving plumes of grass. You can see an important place in our country's history—wide-open land reaching up toward a wide-open sky. ■

(a) Bald eagles nest in large trees near lakes. It takes about five years for eagles to get their white head and tail feathers.

(b) Grasshoppers are plant-eating insects, or herbivores, with long hind legs used for leaping.

(c) Buffalos are large, shaggy-haired animals with horns. Here's one scratching his chin on a rock.

(d) Foxes are flesh-eating animals related to wolves but with smaller and shorter legs and a more pointed muzzle.

The Tallgrass Prairie National Preserve in Kansas was created in 1996 to protect a part of the once vast tallgrass prairie ecosystem.

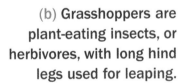

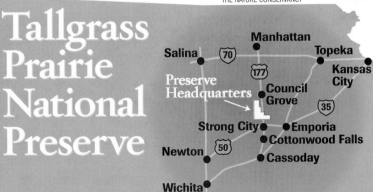

THE NATURE CONSERVANCY

Tallgrass Prairie National Preserve

Salina · Manhattan · Topeka · Kansas City · Preserve Headquarters · Council Grove · Strong City · Emporia · Cottonwood Falls · Newton · Cassoday · Wichita

Covered in Kudzu

Have you ever hidden under a blanket? Do you remember how it felt to be completely covered, from head to toe? After a little while, it was probably hard to breathe in that dark hiding place. And, when you finally threw off the blanket, wasn't it great to breathe the fresh air? What that blanket was doing to you is similar to what a plant, called kudzu, is doing to much of our land!

Kudzu is a vine that smothers other plants under its heavy blanket of leaves. It blocks sunlight from trees, shrubs, and other plants. The weight of the vines can break big branches and bring down tall trees. Kudzu will cover anything in its path—even cars, barns, and houses!

If left alone, kudzu vines can grow 60 feet in just one growing season. That means in a summer, one vine can grow enough to wrap itself around the average car three times! And that's just one vine. Up to 30 vines can grow from a single root. Are you getting the picture? Kudzu is incredible!

Above: Kudzu's growth has been most successful in the southeastern United States due to the nearly ideal growing conditions.

Right: Kudzu vines can grow up to 1 foot (30 cm) a day. Here it is shown taking over a car.

(ALL) COURTESY OF UNITED STATES DEPARTMENT OF AGRICULTURE.

Lots of time and money are spent each growing season to prevent kudzu from taking over. In these pictures, the kudzu is being sprayed with chemicals to kill it.

A Popular Plant Becomes a Pushy Pest

Kudzu is found in many parts of Asia and first came to the United States in 1876 for the country's 100th birthday. The Japanese government planted the leafy, sweet-smelling plant at the Centennial Exposition in Philadelphia, Pennsylvania. A few years later, American nurseries were growing kudzu, and gardeners were planting it in their yards. People loved it! Farmers grew it to feed their animals, and U.S. government workers planted it on hillsides to control erosion.

Because it's an "introduced," or non-native, species, kudzu has few natural enemies in the United States. Insects that feed on kudzu can't slow the plant's growth. Kudzu grows uncontrolled in forests and roadways and places where it was never planted. It grows best where winters are mild, such as the southeastern United States. No wonder that kudzu is sometimes called "the plant that ate the South."

A kudzu flower

Looking for a Few Good Enemies

People have tried many ways to control kudzu. They've cut it, mowed it, burned it, and sprayed it with herbicides, chemicals that kill plants. Scientists have also injected kudzu with a fungus, a tiny organism that takes nutrients from plants. They hope the fungus will weaken the leaves and stems and eventually kill the entire plant—and sometimes it does. In some areas, grazing goats, cows, and sheep keep kudzu from spreading.

Some scientists have traveled to China in search of insects that feed on kudzu. Perhaps they will find an insect that can be safely brought to the United States to help control the plant.

Until kudzu can be stopped, it will keep spreading across the land and threatening native plants and ecosystems. That's because underneath the thick, green kudzu blanket, we know that many different trees, shrubs, and other plants struggle to survive. ■

Weed Warriors Battle Plant Invaders

THE NATURE CONSERVANCY

Mary Travaglini is a Weed Warrior with The Nature Conservancy. She is committed to protecting native plants and trains others in the fight against invasive plants.

THE NATURE CONSERVANCY

Mary Travaglini (say: Trav-a-LEE-nee) is a fighter. It doesn't matter if it's hot or chilly, foggy or clear, Mary goes out and battles her enemies. But she doesn't fight with guns or bombs. She uses other weapons: a saw and a pair of clippers.

Fighting Invasive Plants

You see, Mary is no ordinary soldier. She's a Weed Warrior. She works for The Nature Conservancy, and part of her job is training others to become Weed Warriors, too. Her "weapons" are just what she needs to fight garlic mustard, Japanese stilt grass, kudzu, and other fast-growing invasive plants.

"We need an army to fight against plant invaders," says Mary. "They compete with native plants for light, water, and space, and without our help, the invaders would win. That's because we don't have the insects and diseases that would attack them in their home

The Potomac River Gorge is located about 12 miles outside of Washington, D.C., and is a unique home to many plants and animals.

Japanese stilt grass is an invasive plant that can overgrow native plants by blocking their sunlight and choking their roots.

THE NATURE CONSERVANCY

The *Baptisia australis* or blue wild indigo plant was once used as an antiseptic and is said to keep away flies when grown near farm animals. These plants are being protected by the Weed Warriors of The Nature Conservancy.

THE NATURE CONSERVANCY, R.H. WIEGAND

countries. Without any natural enemies, they can spread and grow quickly."

Mary and her team of volunteer Weed Warriors do battle in the Potomac River Gorge. Only about 12 miles outside of Washington, D.C., the gorge is a beautifully wild place, where 100-year-old trees grow. Wild river oats and blueberries are seen along paths where people love to hike. Several rare plants grow in the gorge as well. "One rare plant, blue wild indigo, is getting smothered by the invasive plants," says Mary.

Helping Wildlife

By pulling out and cutting down invasive plants, the Weed Warriors help not just native plants but also animals. That's because the fruit and seeds of many of the newer plants are not as healthy for birds and other animals as those of native plants.

And so the Weed Warriors eagerly go out to the gorge and battle those pushy vines and shrubs. In their pockets, they carry flash cards with color photos of 'good' and 'bad' plants, in case they get stumped. In a backpack, they carry gloves, and of course, clippers and a saw. Sometimes they have to cut down a shrub as big as their leg!

"I'm sure we are making a difference," says Mary. "But we have to stay at it. We have to protect the native plants here. It's the only way to protect the animals that depend on them for food and shelter. And, it's the only way to save this beautiful natural area, where lots of people love to visit." ■

THE NATURE CONSERVANCY, SUE HENLY

It is hard work removing invasive plants from an area, but Mary Travaglini and the other Weed Warriors believe in protecting the native plants in the Potomac River Gorge.

Plants in Danger

THAT'S A FACT!   Prairies once covered much of central North America, from Texas to Canada. Today, they are found in small protected areas.

I KNOW THAT!   Why is kudzu called "the plant that ate the South"?

WHAT DO YOU THINK?   What do The Nature Conservancy Weed Warriors battle? What are their "weapons"?

HERE'S ONE MORE!   How does the National Collection of Endangered Plants protect plants?

Glossary

Acre: A measure of land area about 4,047 square meters.

Allergy: A reaction to a specific substance that does not bother most people. Some people can be allergic to pollen or peanuts, for example.

Beebread: Nectar and pollen mixed by bees to feed their young

Carnivore: An animal that eats meat.

Chlorophyll: A substance in plants that absorbs light energy. Plants use this energy to make food. Chlorophyll gives green plants their color.

Decomposers: Living things that break down dead plants and animals, and free the nutrients for use by other living things, especially plants.

Ecosystem: A community of plants and animals and the place in which they live. For example, the tallgrass prairie ecosystem.

Endangered plant or animal: One type or group of living things that are close to dying out or becoming extinct.

Epiphyte: A plant that grows attached to something else, usually another plant. Spanish Moss is an epiphyte.

Extinct plant or animal: One type or group of living things that no longer exists or lives.

Geneticist: A scientist who studies how plants or animals pass traits to offspring.

Herbivore: An animal that eats plants.

Hydrophyte: A plant that lives in water, such as a water lily.

Immune system: A group of cells, substances, and other parts of the body that work together to defend the body against foreign invaders.

Landscape architect: A person who plans and designs the use of land.

Nutrient: A substance that is necessary for a plant or animal to grow and live.

Omnivore: An animal that eats both plants and other animals.

Photosynthesis: The process by which green plants, in the presence of light, make food out of carbon dioxide and water.

Pollination: The transfer of pollen from one part of a flower to another part of the same or another flower. This process allows the flower to produce seeds.

Pollinia: Sticky packets of pollen grains found in orchid and milkweed flowers.

Producers: One way to describe plants because they use sunlight to make their own food.

Trait: A unique quality or condition that sets living things apart from one another, and is passed on from parent to offspring, like flower color or eye color.

photo credits